© Ros Ferrara 2017
All rights reserved

Reproduction, storage, adaptation or translation, in any form or by any means, of this publication is prohibited without the prior written permission of the publisher. Excerpts may be reproduced for the purpose of research, private study, criticism or review, or by educational institutions solely for educational purposes, without permission, providing full acknowledgement is given.

First Published in the UK in 2017 by Focus Education (UK) Ltd

Focus Education (UK) Ltd
Publishing
Talking Point Conference & Exhibition Centre
Huddersfield Road
Scouthead
Saddleworth
OL4 4AG

Focus Education (UK) Ltd Reg. No 4507968

ISBN 978-1-911416-12-8

Companies, institutions and other organisations wishing to make bulk purchases of books published by Focus Education should contact their local bookstore or Focus Education direct:

Customer Services, Focus Education, Talking Point Conference & Exhibition Centre,
Huddersfield Road, Scouthead, Saddleworth, OL4 4AG
Tel 01457 821818 Fax 01457 878205

www.focus-education.co.uk
customerservice@focus-education.co.uk
Printed in Great Britain by Focus Education UK Ltd, Scouthead

CW01642734

About the author

Ros Ferrara is a full-time consultant with Focus Education. Much of her recent work has been on developing all aspects of English in the current curriculum.

Prior to joining Focus, Ros worked in a consultancy and advisory role for Lambeth LA. During this period, she led development work on the National Strategies highly successful EAL Programme, was the Literacy lead for the authority and Primary Strategy Manager. Ros led and managed a range of initiatives, including Every Child a Reader, Every Child a Writer and action research aimed at improving writing. Her role also involved working very closely with senior leaders in schools on developing leadership, improving the quality of teaching and other school improvement issues.

Recent feedback:

Very professional: we had confidence in her judgements.

Style was relaxed and approachable. Good balance between listening and practical activities.

Ros was wonderful. The material was relevant and interesting. Ros's presentation skills were excellent. Her interactions with teachers were professional but relaxed.

Ros has transformed writing in the school.

The support received both by senior leaders, middle managers and classroom practitioners has been key to our becoming an outstanding school.

The consultancy Ros has given to my school has empowered my staff and the impact is already notable when I look at pupil outcomes.

(c) Focus Education (UK) Ltd

Contents

(c) Focus Education (UK) Ltd

Introduction

It is clearly understood that standards in writing in the current curriculum are raised and that all writing needs to be effective, impact on the reader and be accurate. For all pupils, to meet the expected standard at the end of each year is the aim of all teachers. This, in itself requires highly effective and reflective teaching.

In addition, there remains the scope for pupils to demonstrate that they are working at greater depth within the expected standard. Official guidance for this is lacking both in substance and clarity. This is available only for Year 2 and Year 6 and in Year 2 refers only to punctuation, spelling and handwriting.

The children who are judged to be writing at greater depth are children who stand out as writers. They are the children who take our breath away when we read their texts. There will not be many of these children and the number will vary from cohort to cohort. Whilst we cannot "teach" children to be greater depth writers, we can most certainly offer them opportunities, choices and ensure that any technical aspects of writing are secure and their use understood.

The recent publication of a new updated assessment framework for judging writing at the end of Year 2 and Year 6 has a welcome focus on composition and effect and the impact on the intended reader. Whilst the more technical aspects of writing are included, the shift is towards how they are being used rather than that they have been included.

In addition, the expectation that children will use models from their reading and draw on real writers' techniques to use in their writing is made explicit.

Thanks to the staff and children at Shibden Head Primary Academy, Freehold Primary Academy, Milton Primary School and St. Mary's RC Primary School, Chesterfield for the writing samples.

Recognising Potential

What could we expect to see? Children who:

- read with a writer's eye, noticing the effects a writer creates and asking how he or she did it
- master handwriting and spelling – these skills need to be automatic so that children are not too preoccupied with them to concentrate on composition
- know what they want to say – pupils need reasons to write, and suitable content to write about
- internalise the different stages of the writing process: planning, drafting and editing and proof reading their work
- write with a reader's eye, constantly re-reading work to check that it makes sense and that the message is effectively conveyed
- know how different sorts of texts are structured, so that, over time, they can create their own structures appropriate to audience and purpose
- have a feeling for grammar, varying and controlling sentence structure with ease, in order to create different language effects
- are capable of writing at length while maintaining a sense of audience, purpose and organisation

(c) Focus Education (UK) Ltd

From early on, children's writing may:

- have a strong awareness of audience
- pay attention to the craft of writing
- show an original style or "voice"
- show an ability to imitate or experiment with different styles of writing
- show an awareness of more sophisticated language and literary features and consciously use them
- apply reading experiences to writing
- show a dislike of repetitive, closed or over-scaffolded tasks

Understanding Needs

What do these pupils need?

- To read a wide and varied range of high quality literature, including non-fiction
- To participate in in-depth discussion of literature to understand the writer's craft
- To be taught key features and be shown how writers use them
- To be encouraged to have an awareness and interest in words and language
- Opportunities to experiment with writing and language
- Opportunities to make choices about audience, purpose, style and structure of writing
- Opportunities to develop their own success criteria or toolkits for writing
- Time to write at length if appropriate
- To understand that they are writing to create impact and effect their chosen reader
- Time to evaluate, re-draft, edit and proof read with the understanding that a first draft is only the beginning of the writing process
- Writing conversations with peers and with adults

What should be avoided?

- Devised lists of success criteria with features to be included in writing
- Over- scaffolding, including too much imitation or superficial innovation
- Use of manufactured texts which aim to exemplify particular technical skills
- Closed, over-structured tasks
- Insufficient focus or time on evaluating, drafting, editing and proof reading

(c) Focus Education (UK) Ltd

Year 1

(c) Focus Education (UK) Ltd

Year 1 Writers working at greater depth

Year 1 writers working at greater depth use and apply the Year 1 learning independently in different contexts. They write recounts, which are chronologically organised, related to other curriculum areas – history, geography, science, R.E. Writing follows a logical order, linking events and ideas. They write narratives using some of the key narrative language from stories they know. They can open a narrative by describing a character, rather than writing about an event and narratives have a clear opening, middle and ending. They can sustain the writing of longer texts which hold the interest of the reader. Sentences are accurately constructed with capital letters and the correct end punctuation to indicate statements, questions or exclamations. They write more extended sentences experimenting with different conjunctions and different ways of starting sentences – pronouns rather than nouns, adverbs. They actively seek and use new words in their writing, including precisely chosen nouns and adjectives and technical words as appropriate. These writers make plausible attempts at spelling new words, using the phonic knowledge from Year 1. They also spell the common exception words from Year 1 and beyond accurately. Letters are correctly formed and oriented with ascenders and descenders and capital and lower case letters evident.

(c) Focus Education (UK) Ltd

Foot prints in the snow

One snowy morning a Mr Nice wolf sat by the burning fire reading all the books he had about wolves. All the wolves in the stories were nasty scary and greedy. Mr Nice wolf said I think its time someone wrote a story about a nice wolf he said so he went to his brown and dusty tabel and he started to write a story with his black silver pen and this is how the story began. One snowy evning it snowed and snowed and snowed when it finlly stoped snowing a Mr Nice wolf steped out of his house and went for a walk. Then he spotted some foot prints in the icy cold smooth glittery snow. Hmm I wonder whose those could be he said so he folowed the footprints into the forest. One minit later he saw a growing red squirrel in the tree top. Exkuse maden are these footprints yours he asked the squirrel politly. No, why do you ask. I want to find out so that I can make a new friend he said. And with that he scampered back into his tree trunk house. A little while later he spotted a rabbit hole. Out came a bunny poking her nose out of her burrow. Exkuse me maden are these foot prints yours he said. No, why would you ask because I want to make a new friend. And with that he hopped back into his burow to look of his wifes baby rabbits. Mr Nice wolf tried to ignor what he said and caryon. One minit later he spotted a big blue lake

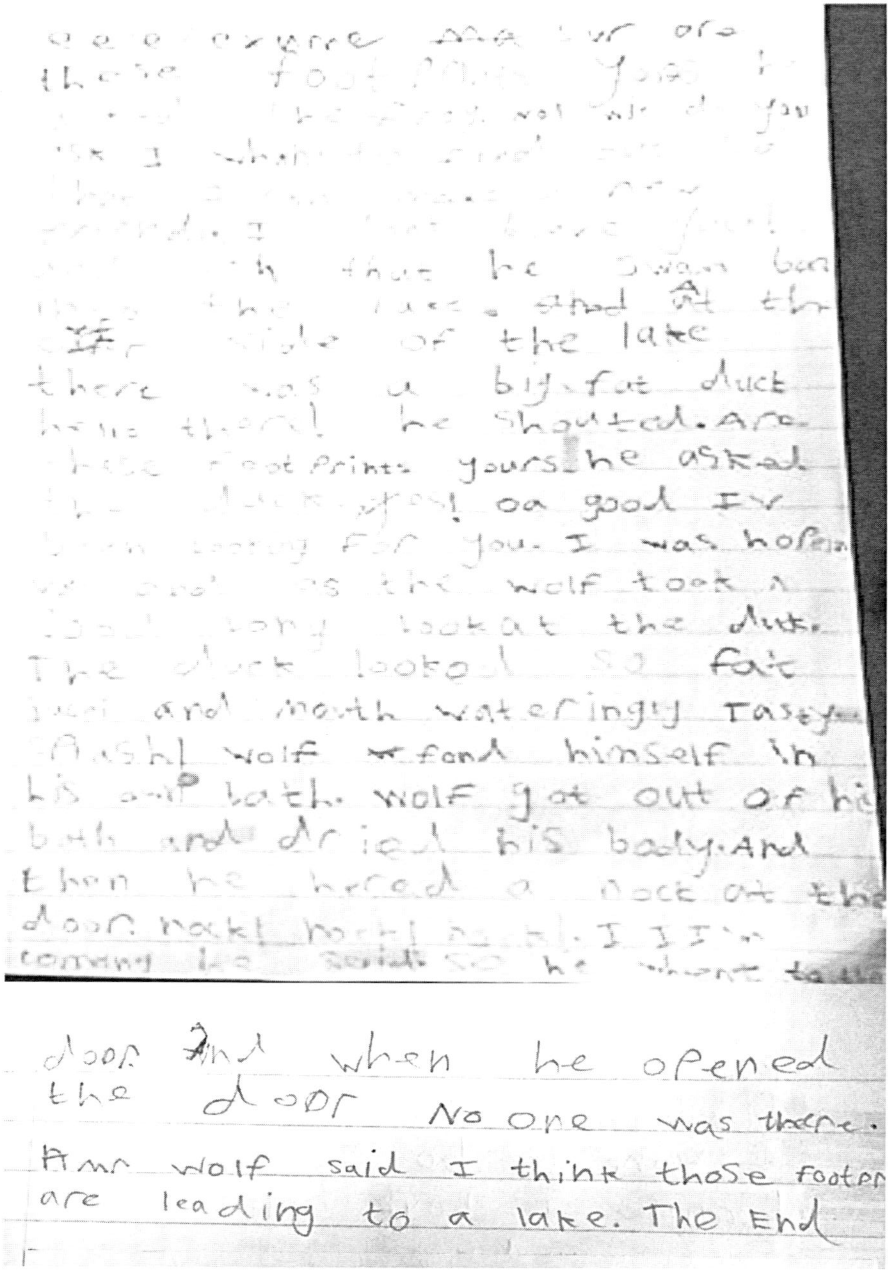

This Year 1 pupil clearly demonstrates greater depth writing in the sample.

A narrative retold in full, drawing on the language from the text as well as some thoughtful additions. The writing is sustained and has a clear ending, based on the original ending.

The writing took place following several weeks of exploring the book, discussing it and orally retelling the story. Work on word choices – precise nouns, verbs and adjectives – as well as work on sentence structure was also covered.

The children were given as much time, over several days, as they needed to complete the task.

In addition, there had been specific modelling of how to evaluate and edit and proof read work. At this point – late February – the pupil was able to independently evaluate their writing using a pink pen and to identify where changes were needed in green and make them.

Working with Year 1 potential greater depth writers:

- Encourage wide reading and make explicit links and connections with other reading experiences
- Discuss the use of language and word choices made by the writer
- Collect words from reading
- Plan for the retelling of stories for most of the year rather than making changes. This will enable the focus to be on the quality of language and the use of narrative language patterns
- Similarly, plan for the recounting of actual events and experiences with the focus on language choices and content – what does the reader want to know?
- Develop vocabulary and discuss word choices, being clear about which words may not be suitable. Focus on precise choices of nouns, adjectives and verbs
- Have a relentless focus on sentence structure and the concept of a sentence and correct punctuation
- Raise awareness of different ways to start sentences
- Make explicit and model the importance of accuracy
- Towards the end of the year, give opportunities for children to make a change to a story or to write about an invented character or a changed setting
- Teach the children how to evaluate their writing and guide them as they develop editing and proof reading skills. However, make it clear that this process takes place after composition

(c) Focus Education (UK) Ltd

Year 2

Year 2 Writers at Greater Depth

Year 2 writers working at greater depth write longer texts which maintain the purpose of the text type whenever they are writing, including in other curriculum areas. Narratives are clearly structured and have an ending which relates to the main character. Dialogue is usually included in narrative writing with speech marks used accurately. Non-narrative texts are organised and laid out appropriately and related material is grouped into sections with some attempts at paragraphing. Word choices are more precise with specific nouns and well-chosen adjectives which are often drawn from their reading. Some literary devices such as similes and alliteration are used for effect. Expanded noun phrases are used to add detail for effect and go beyond the simple addition of an adjective. They use a range of sentence starters which may also be drawn from their reading. This will include some adverbials which move events on in a narrative. Punctuation taught so far is used to ensure that meaning is clear. Spelling is mostly accurate with plausible errors in more ambitious word choices. These writers discuss the effectiveness of their writing and may make changes without prompting.

Pupils need to meet the statements in the 2017-2018 assessment framework on the following page.

2017-2018 Assessment Frameworks

Working at the expected standard	Working at greater depth
The pupil can, after discussion with the teacher: • write simple, coherent narratives about personal experiences and those of others (real or fictional) • write about real events, recording these simply and clearly • demarcate most sentences in their writing with capital letters and full stops, and use question marks correctly when required • use present and past tense mostly correctly and consistently • use co-ordination (e.g. or / and / but) and some subordination (e.g. when / if / that / because) to join clauses • segment spoken words into phonemes and represent these by graphemes, spelling many of these words correctly and making phonically-plausible attempts at others • spell many common exception words • form capital letters and digits of the correct size, orientation and relationship to one another and to lower-case letters • use spacing between words that reflects the size of the letters.	The pupil can, after discussion with the teacher: • write effectively and coherently for different purposes, drawing on their reading to inform the vocabulary and grammar of their writing • make simple additions, revisions and proof-reading corrections to their own writing • use the punctuation taught at key stage 1 mostly correctly • spell most common exception words • add suffixes to spell most words correctly in their writing (e.g. –ment, –ness, –ful, –less, –ly) • use the diagonal and horizontal strokes needed to join some letters.

(c) Focus Education (UK) Ltd

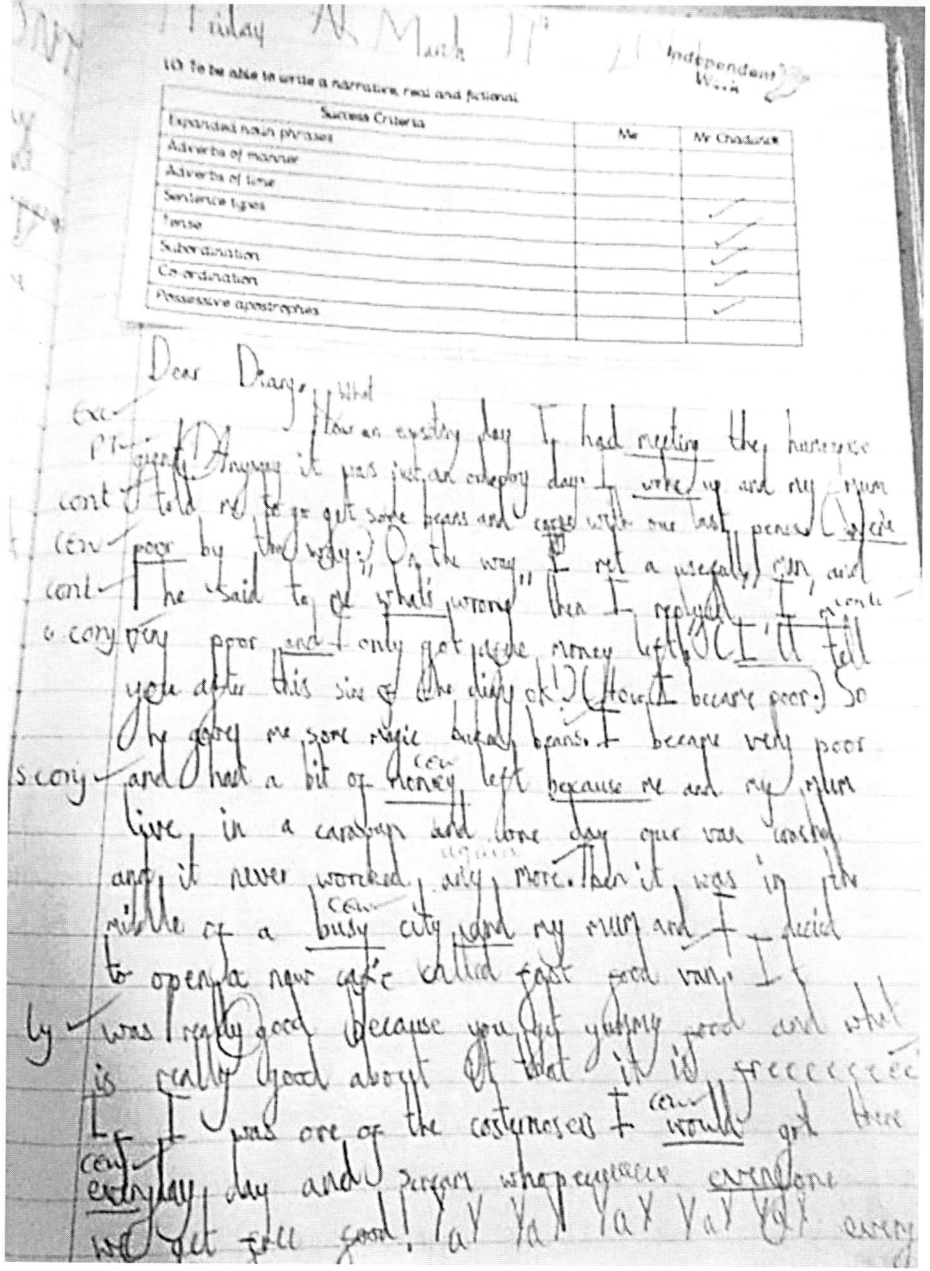
LO: To be able to write a narrative, real and fictional
Success Criteria
Me
Expanded noun phrases
Adverbs of manner
Adverbs of time
Sentence types
Tense
Subordination
Co-ordination
Possessive apostrophes

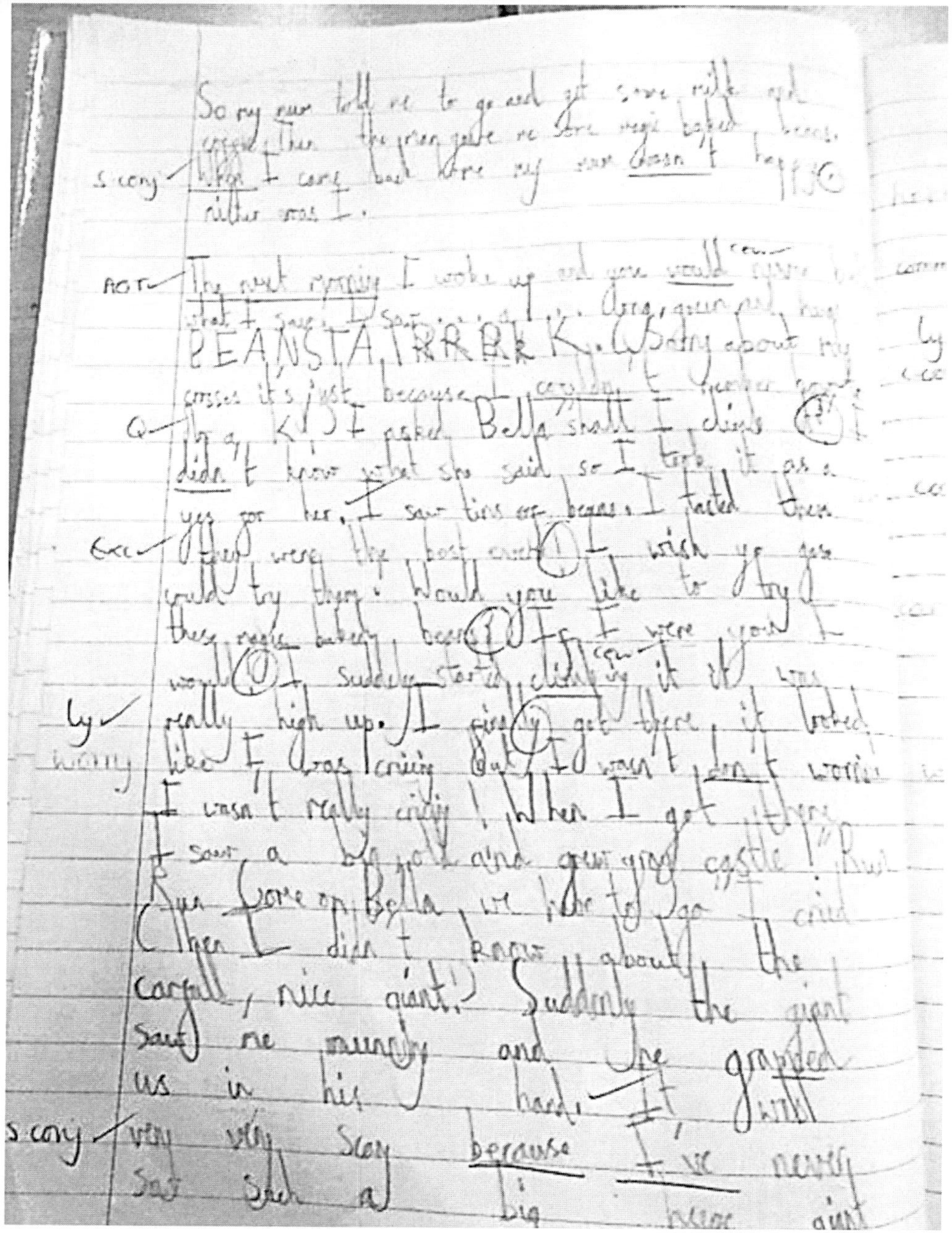

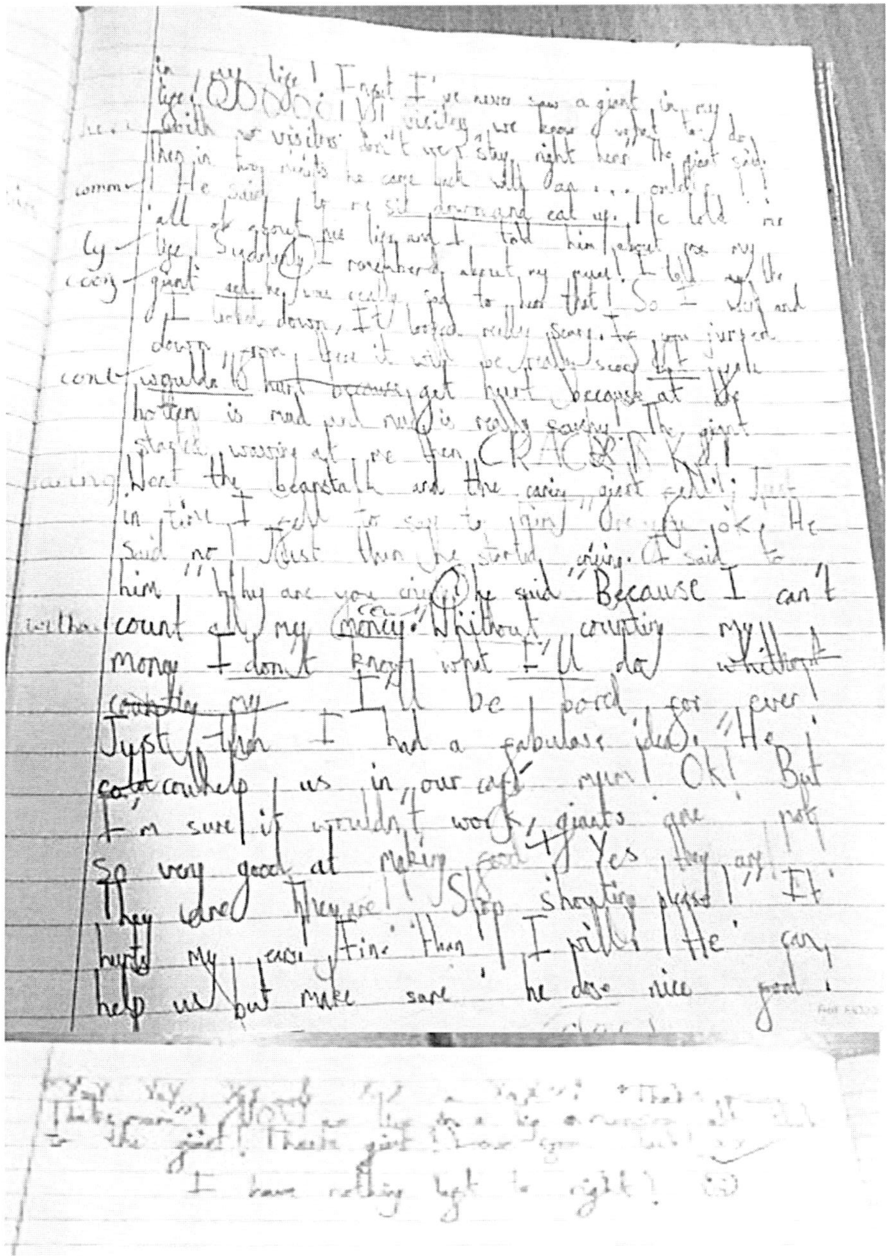

This Year 2 pupil clearly demonstrates greater depth writing in the sample.
The task required in depth understanding of the events and the ability to empathise with and take on the role of the character in order to write in the first person.
The text is sustained and shows originality and a clear voice throughout. All the requirements of the Year 2 curriculum are evident and writing is mostly accurately spelled and punctuated. The writing is beginning to show the use of paragraphing.
Sentences are well-controlled and word choices are appropriate and carefully chosen. Time adverbials are selected to move events forward and make the reader aware of the passing of time. There is also evidence of language drawn from reading.
A purple pen has ben used to edit and proof read independently, showing awareness of inaccuracies and changes for impact.

Working with Year 2 potential greater depth writers:

- Encourage wide reading and make explicit links and connections with other reading experiences
- Discuss the use of language and word choices made by the writer and collect examples for use in writing
- Plan for opportunities to adapt or change an element of a narrative or to write in the first person. By the end of the year, discuss possible changes or adaptations and offer choice
- Explore paragraphing and develop understanding of how to group material in non-narrative writing and how a paragraph in a narrative can signal change
- Develop vocabulary and discuss word choices, being clear about which words may not be suitable. Focus on how to add detail by expanding noun phrases in different ways, by using powerful verbs and well-chosen adverbs
- Widen and explore the meaning of the range of conjunctions used and the use of the subordinate clause at the beginning of a sentence
- Experiment with, evaluate and use some literary techniques for impact: power of three, similes, different sentence starters
- Emphasis the importance of planning
- Ensure that proof reading checklists are used independently for all writing and the importance of accuracy is understood
- Develop independent editing and proof reading skills

Year 3

(c) Focus Education (UK) Ltd

Year 3 Writers at Greater Depth

Year 3 writers working at greater depth are beginning to make choices about the appropriate style of writing for their purpose. The impact of their reading is reflected in their writing. Narratives are very well structured and have a clear ending which directly relates to the beginning. Paragraphing is clear and clearly show the difference between different events or information. Writing is carefully planned and annotated with precise word choices. Greater emphasis is given to the use and choice of verbs and adverbs to add detail to events, settings and characters. They automatically choose the appropriate text type for their purpose from those taught and write with increasing awareness of their reader, actively attempting to engage them. Sentence structures taught are used confidently and sentence starters show greater variety, including the use of adverbials of time and place. Punctuation addressed so far is used accurately to ensure meaning is clear. Writing is edited; changes are made to create greater impact on the reader and proof-read for accuracy.

Once upon a time, there was a little boy named Hansel and his younger sister, Gretel. The two children lived in a dreary shack in a dreary wood with their Father, who was a Woodman. The woodman had a wife but she died years ago, so he married a new person but she wasn't as nice, and that was how the trouble began. The new wife was Hansel and Gretel's Stepmother. She wanted to get rid of the children due to the fact she was jealous of the two children and she wanted the Woodman's love more than the two children.

One misty night, the stepmother told her husband "Dump the children into the forest, so they may never come back!" shouted the stepmother angrily. The Woodman disagreed with his wife so she raged and raved all day until he would agree with her. Finally, the woodman took them in the forest for the first time. Hansel overheard the stepmother's idea so he gathered shiny white pebbles before ⊛ went into the deep, dark woods. A few hours later, it was midnight and the Woodman started to take Hansel and Gretel into the forest. He said that they were going to help him to chop some wood so he took them into the gloomiest corners of the woods. Hansel knew that his father was faking and this was just so they couldn't get back, but Hansel had dropped pebbles on his way to the fores "Stay here while I go and collect some firewood!" lied the Woodman. As the full moon rose up, tears rolled down Gretel's cheeks. "Where's Dad?" said Gretel, in a worried voice "Don't worry." Said Hansel, cheerfully. "All we need to do is follow the trail of pebbles

"What do you mean?" asked Gretel. "I left a trail of white pebbles on our way to the forest, because the Stepmother was telling Dad to dump us into the forest so we can't get back." replied Hansel. "Wait! What?" said Gretel. "Um, never mind," said Hansel. "Let's just follow the trail."

The next morning, Hansel and Gretel were back to the little house. They ran to the Woodman in joy. Their hearts leaped up to the moon! "Dad!" shouted Hansel and Gretel together. "Sweetpies!" shouted the Woodman, joyfully. The Woodman was shocked, the two children had come back. "Gah!" "How did they come back?!" thought the wicked Stepmother. The Stepmother started to rage and rave again. The Woodman started to take them in the forest again. This time was different though. Hansel had no time to gather white stones that gleamed the Sun/Moonlight, so he gathered tiny bread crumbs instead. At nightfall Hansel dropped the breadcrumbs. As the fullmoon had taken over the sun, Hansel's hands started to sweat as it got darker and darker and darker. At sunrise, Hansel woke up and couldn't see any signs of breadcrumbs. There was only one left. When they least expected it, a bird came and ate the last breadcrumb. "Oh dear," thought Hansel. All the birds must of ate all of the trail. All of a sudden, Gretel woke up. "You look very tired," said Hansel. "It's just... I stayed up for a long time... and I went to sleep at 1am," yawned Gretel, slowly. "Well, I can't find a trail, but I did leave one!" explained Hansel. "The birds ate all of the trail!"

(+) Add show not tell for how they looked.

~~The Woodman looked~~ said Gretel in a confused voice.

"Hey bird!" shouted Gretel, Loudly. "You've ate all of the trail!" Surprisingly, the bird started to speak! "Let me show you to your house because I know you're trying to get back to it!" howled the owl, who was not as good as his word.

As they followed the riddling owl, they were shocked out of their skin that they had seen a house made of candy! Something was strange though. This wasn't their house! They turned back to speak to the owl, but he dissapeared. Something was getting strange around here. They've found a candy house and now the owl's dissapeared. Then, Hansel and Gretel started to taste the house. The candy wasn't fake. Suddenly, out popped a green nose. Who would have a green nose? The creaky, wooden, door opened... An old woman stood before them. She sniffed the two children. Who would sniff children?! "Come in, dearies," said the old woman, in a welcoming voice. "You must have some tea, dearies!" said the old woman, politely. She brung the jelly for extra treatment. Soon, the children were offered soft beds to sleep in. When they fell asleep, the old woman snatched Hansel and took him downstairs to a whole room that Hansel and Gretel never knew about. She threw him into a tiny cold cellar for a child to live in. The lock went clunk!

The Witch climbed up back upstairs to snatch Gretel away as well. She told her to work and cook Hansel up, but Gretel had a plan. The old woman didn't pretend to be nice anymore. She was a witch all along. The Witch told Hansel she was going to fatten him up for her dinner, so he better get used to the idea. This was Gretel's chance to act. "Stupid fire!" shouted Gretel. "This thing won't work!" "Let me see," said the Witch. Gretel knew that the Witch couldn't see that well and that was part of the plan. The Witch looked closer. PUSH! The Witch fell into the oven and Gretel shut the metal door! The oven roared as if it was fired with magic coal. The house began to shake. "You'll never get from me!" shrieked the Witch angrily. As quick as a flash, Gretel unlocked the prison door. "Let's get out of here!" shouted Gretel.

Like a bolt of lightning, they escaped from the little house quickly. As they escaped, tons of gold fell from the icing rooftop and on their way home Hansel collected some of the treasure. "Hansel, come on!" shouted Gretel hurriedly. "Wait there! Maybe we should collect some of the treasure," suggested Hansel. "I've got enough now anyway, so let's go!" BOOM! BANG! went the house again and again.

A very clear voice is evident with a good understanding of the language required for a traditional narrative. Purpose and audience are established and sustained throughout the text. Events are sequenced and developed.
Characters are well-developed by using action, dialogue and "show and not tell".
Evidence of effective paragraphing with changes of time particularly evident.
Sentence structure is generally well-controlled with simple, compound and complex sentences being used to add flow and cohesion to the text. Some evidence of multi-clause sentences although these are sometimes too long and lack clarity. Sentence openings are varied.
Word choices are precise; language has been chosen which is appropriate to the narrative genre. Expanded noun phrases help to create a picture for the reader.
Conjunctions, adverbs and prepositions are used to sequence and to express place and cause confidently.

First and third person and tenses are used consistently and accurately.

Punctuation is accurate, including the punctuation of dialogue.

Working with Year 3 potential greater depth writers:

- Encourage wide reading and make explicit links and connections with other reading experiences
- Discuss the use of language and word choices made by the writer and collect examples for use in writing
- Plan for opportunities to discuss how a written task might be adapted or changed and offer choices
- Develop paragraphing and the understanding of the topic sentence in a paragraph which introduces the reader to the content of the paragraph or marks a change in time or place
- Develop the use of dialogue to show character, including the choice of the dialogue verb
- Develop the technique of "show and not tell" to develop character and to show characters' feelings
- Explore different ways to start sentences and why they might be used
- Develop vocabulary and discuss word choices. Explore synonyms and shades of meaning within them
- Experiment with different sentence types and how and why they are used to create flow in writing or particular effects.
- Experiment with, evaluate and use some literary techniques, drawn from reading, for impact; for example, alliteration, onomatopoeia, metaphor
- Offer support to develop own success criteria or toolkits
- Have regular writing conversations throughout the writing process with a focus on evaluating the impact of writing and developing understanding that a first draft needs reflection and evaluation
- Develop independent editing and proof reading skills

(c) Focus Education (UK) Ltd

Year 4

(c) Focus Education (UK) Ltd

Year 4 Writers at Greater Depth

Year 4 writers working at greater depth demonstrate good awareness of the audience for their writing and choose vocabulary and structures for their purpose and to engage and impact on their identified reader. Word choices are well-considered and may be used to build a description, an event, tension or emotion. Technical vocabulary is used purposefully in non-narrative writing. Writing demonstrates an unconscious understanding of the use of formal and informal language dependent on the purpose and audience. Different sentence types and varied word order are used to create specific effects. Paragraphing is clear and ideas are developing and linked to guide the reader through the text. Writing usually has a clear voice which is sustained through both shorter and more extended texts. Clear links with reading are made with writers, using models from their reading to construct sentences and paragraphs and the editing process draws explicitly on this.

(c) Focus Education (UK) Ltd

sp The harbour was filled with ghostly shadows
sp that seemed to consume Fravia in the mist. Every so
often pale vapour clouds hooked themselves onto
the little girl's frozen head, making her shiver
sp even more violently than before. The creaking
floorboards under Fravia's feet seemed to whisper
every time she trod on them. "You're ours now!"
they said in a ancient voice. In the flickering
torchlight, she could make out a twisting and
turning path that was liable to break at any
movement. (XI) (at any moment) at any moment. Captain Genning's
lo father had warned her against ever journeying this
but now that she was there there was no turning

The harbour light did little to add to her vision
and her lively imagination thought of herself walking
straight off the edge. She could feel the veil
of icy mist consuming her more and more as she paced
the way up to the main dock. Every step she took
was an effort and she wished she could lie down.
Billowing grey mist filled the harbour, making
it worse. The sinister storehouses loomed over her
like ghosts with no home. The dark doorway was the open
mouth of a giant waiting to eat her. Frightened,
Fravia hurried on past the gloomy storage warehouses
and the (the large objects that seemed to swallow her) cold immense bridges past the berthing sites.
Suddenly a ghostly figure appeared (XI) on the
mist. He had short white scars, an injured face and
a pale face. This man... This man. This man was
remarkable.

In the dark forest tunnell, not a whisper could be heard. There was not even the quiet twit of a bird and the quiet autumn scene was frozen in a flash of stillness. In the middle of that beatiful picture, I, Charlie Small was sitting on a water tight raft, having of being in possession of only a small rucksack which contained all I needed. Well. All I needed for a normal adventure. At that very moment something nudged my raft. "Fish," I thought but little did I know that I couldn't be more wrong...

Slowly, I rocked on and off the raft, fighting to stay on. But the circumstances were tough and I soon gave in, falling into the choppy current below. I could not feel my legs nor my heart as I felt my mind think the last thoughts that I would ever think. Just as I thought that I would suffocate underneath the murky depths, a deafening crunch snapped me

I didn't know which way was up. In great panick, I kicked my legs into and surfaced glimpsing a set of jumbo sized teeth. I knew what I h to do but it sounded almost madman to me. Ignoring the feeling o fear in my gut, I did a large jump onto the reptiles huge back and we off on a ride making my head burst and whirling until I couldn seek in another breath, even if we were above water.

Suddenly, we broke the surface and the scenery around us blu in a flash of green and yellows. Birds stopped twitting, foxes sto hunting. This was a proper battle. The crocodile knocked against my head and for a moment I suspected to feel the row of sharp teet the crocodile bite into my neck but instead I heard a soft crunching sound backpack had saved me.

Slowly I had a brainstorm. Like clockwork, my sweaty hand r out for my string. Suddenly, my hand reached out for the t in my bag. In my plan the string was a lifesaver and I the victim.

Terrified and exited, I numbly hoisted myself onto the l beast's back. Almost breaking my back in the process, I shimmie the night mare's back and tied some string around its mou. Knowing my life was at stake, I jumped and grabbed the st for dear life, pulling it tight.

I wrestled the croc, it biting savagely at me but then, on distance I saw the flying start of a... Waterfall. I tried stop but it was too late. I washed over the point of no return then... Thump.

(c) Focus Education (UK) Ltd

In both samples, writing demonstrates an awareness of the reader; it is engaging and maintains the reader's interest. The texts are well-developed and well-paced. The pace is varied as atmosphere and tension is built. The purpose of the texts is clear.

Paragraphs are well-structured, aid cohesion and guide the reader through the text. Topic sentences clearly indicate change in time, place or event. Fronted adverbials are used appropriately and effectively to support this.

Sentences are mostly well-structured and include the more controlled use of multi-clause sentences. Range of sentences types is used confidently and appropriately according to the purpose and audience.

They are opened in different ways to create effects, including the positioning of clauses and the use of fronted adverbials and to support the cohesion of the text.

Characters are developed through show and not tell techniques, using their actions, speech, thoughts and reactions.

Pronouns are used to avoid repetition and to support cohesion across the text.

Word choices are deliberate and thoughtful. Carefully thought-out detail is added with noun phrases which are expanded before and after the noun with adjectives, prepositional phrases, adverbial phrases. This adds interest, creates atmosphere, builds tension and engages the reader.

Punctuation is accurate with commas used correctly for fronted adverbials, embedded phrases and clauses, as well as for the reporting clause in dialogue.

(c) Focus Education (UK) Ltd

Working with Year 4 potential greater depth writers:

- Encourage wide reading and make explicit links and connections with other reading experiences
- Discuss the use of language and word choices made by the writer and collect examples for use in writing
- Investigate and discuss different writer's styles and techniques. Experiment with writing in the style of…
- Offer and discuss choices about how to undertake a task
- Explore how paragraphing is used to structure different text types and raise awareness that paragraphs may be of very varied lengths
- Explore how ideas, content or information is linked within a paragraph and evaluate and review own writing for links
- Develop the use of dialogue, action and description to show character and to move events forward
- Develop sentence starters by adding detail
- Experiment with word choices. Find synonyms and antonyms and discuss meanings and the appropriate use.
- Encourage independent exploration of words
- Experiment with different sentence lengths to vary pace
- Experiment with, evaluate and use some literary techniques, drawn from reading, for impact; for example, alliteration, onomatopoeia, metaphor
- Encourage more independent development of their own success criteria or toolkits
- Have regular writing conversations throughout the writing process with a focus on evaluating the impact of writing and developing understanding that a first draft needs reflection and evaluation
- Develop independent editing and proof reading skills

Year 5

(c) Focus Education (UK) Ltd

Year 5 Writers working at greater depth

Year 5 writers working at greater depth write texts in different contexts across the curriculum with clear purpose and audience. Writing is clearly structured and organised according to the text type. They attempt to write hybrid texts to show an alternative point of view or to engage the reader with an unexpected approach. The use of Standard English is consistent and level of formality appropriate for the register of the text. Paragraphs are clearly constructed and help to guide the reader through the text. Those in narrative writing support the plot structure and clearly signal changes in time, place and events. Paragraphs consistently open with topic sentences setting out the main idea which is then developed. In all writing the closing of a text refers to the opening. They adapt sentence structures by re-ordering or embedding clauses and use different sentence lengths to create effects. Detail is often added by expanding noun phrases and sentence starters with effective word choices. Commas are used accurately to mark grammatical boundaries and proof reading checks that they help to clarify intended meaning. The editing process may involve taking out or simplifying rather than adding.

AT

Hear, and listen well, my friends, for I will tell you a tale that takes us back to the troubles and terrors of the fifth century in Angleland. A tale which has been told for thousands of years.

Our Angle ancestors was ruled by a fair, kind king. King Cerdic, who proved he was a mighty warrior, made Angleland happy and prosperous. The people of Angleland were safe in their homes, warm at their hearths and were well fed.

The kingdom was a peaceful place. King Cerdic had many successful victories in battle and he brought back several treasures from his perilous journeys. This made the people of his kingdom elated. This made Angleland truly a land of sweet content.

To celebrate the preposprity of the kingdom, Cerdic announced that there was going to be a feast at the marvellous mead-hall, where they could be enthralled and enraptured in happiness of the poet's stories. Angleland was a flourishing kingdom of happiness.

But this peace and kindness didn't last forever. /

T

One terrifying, fateful night, a savage, cruel monster roamed the kingdom. However, this creature wasn't like any creature. He was a beast born of evil. As he stormed towards the mead-hall, a dark shadow covered Angleland. The sound of joyous laughter got louder and louder, echoing around the hall. It was hateful to his ears, it was more than his evil heart could bear.

Enraged with fury, he burst open the doors of the mead-hall, aggresively. Screams of terror filled the room. That night, he slaughtered many, causing lots of destruction. He was a flesh-eating beast, showing no mercy. This merciless monster swallowed them all in one big gulp.

This happened for 12 long months. The people lived in grief and despair as every night was an endless terror. The mead-hall was empty and stayed empty. Even King Cerdic's fiercest warriors didn't stand a chance at this hellish, demonic fiend. Now, joyous laughter was replaced with screams of terror and horror. They lived a dreadful tragetty, a hideous nightmare. A rule of terror was upon Angleland.

the gruesome, gorging Jabberwock. He just didn't stand a chance.

So in those 12 months of murder and slaughter, he sent messages across the seas, asking for help. The Jabberwock was taking away happiness from his kingdom. They needed a warrior, a hero to save them.

Across the seas was the warrior, Beowulf. In the land of the Geats, he was the most brave and daring the kingdom had ever seen. When Beowulf heard about the terrifying troubles in Angleland, he didn't hesitate one bit. There was no time to loose. Beowulf, who was a strong fighter, chose the bravest of warriors for the perilous mission and set sail.

On the stormed-tossed ocean, the boat rocked side to side, back and forth. On the wind-whipped waves, he sailed towards Angleland. As the kingdom came to sight, they thanked God for their safe journey.

Weary now from their long sea journey, Beowulf and his mighty brothers-in-arms marched up the rocky, cliff hill towards King Cerdic's mead-hall. As they approached it, it was already dark and they caught sight of the Jabberwock. They peered closer. They watched as he gobbled up people.

Knowing that it was the right time, Beowulf let go of an arrow, aimed directly for the monster of the dark shadows. The Jabberwock shot his eyes at that very moment in Beowulf's direction. They didn't move. Troublesome, trecherous - the Jabberwock let out a mighty roar.

Beowulf bravely ran up to the Jabberwock and pounced on his back like a vicious tiger pouncing on it's prey. Brave Beowulf got hold of the Jabberwock's arm and squeezed it as tight as he probably could (it was that tight).

The merciless, murderous ogre let out a screech as loud as an elephant blowing it's trunk. As he was in agony, his roar was endless and the terrible noise was resounding through Angleland. Battling Beowulf fought on, battling for victory, battling for peace upon Angleland, to restore love and kindness to the kingdom.

Now, Beowulf knew that it was

nearly the end of this vile and vengeful creature. Gnawing and gnashing, Beowulf summoned the last of strength. Anger only made him stronger. He pinned the gore and gluttonous fiend and he leaked fiendish blood.

As the Jabberwock fell to the ground, King Cerdic came running and praising Beowulf. He said, "Thank you! You are a deathdyfing champion deafeating this living nightmare. I will reward you with many treasures as you have returned love and kindness to my kingdom. I don't know how else to thank you."

And that's how it stayed. Angleland was truly a land of sweet content once again. It was a kingdom of kindness.

One word, brilliant! 

Writing for an audience is evident and the purpose is made clear. The reader is addressed directly and a specific style, drawn from reading, adopted and sustained throughout the text. The plot is well-developed, paced and sequenced with an engaging opening and effective closing.

Paragraphs are well-controlled and shape the text, guiding the reader effectively through shifts in time and place and changes of events or information. Topic sentences are used to introduce the main idea of the paragraph as well as establish links across paragraphs. Within paragraphs, ideas are developed and well sequenced.

The setting creates atmosphere and mood, and is also used to indicate changes in atmosphere and mood.

Simple, compound and complex sentences used to extend meaning and add variety and interest as appropriate and for the purpose and audience of the writing, as well as to impact on the reader. Expanded phrases and clauses are used to add information or detail appropriate to the purpose and audience, including relative clauses.

Words are carefully and deliberately selected and used precisely to clarify meaning, enhance effect, increase/slow pace and create mood. Word choices reflect the purpose and style of the text.

Writing is highly accurate with commas used correctly to clarify meaning.

(c) Focus Education (UK) Ltd

Working with Year 5 potential greater depth writers:

- Encourage wide reading and make explicit links and connections with other reading experiences
- Discuss the use of language and word choices made by the writer and collect examples for use in writing
- Widen range of different writers' styles and techniques investigated, discussed and used as a base for writing.
- Encourage, discuss and experiment with the adaptation of the features of different text types for the purpose or audience for the writing
- Identify and discuss viewpoint in reading and use knowledge to establish and maintain a clear viewpoint in writing
- Develop understanding of informal and formal language and their appropriate use
- Develop understanding of direct and reported speech and its effective use
- Develop understanding of cohesion and flow within and between paragraphs
- Understand and experiment with different verb forms and control them within multi-clause sentences
- Encourage independent exploration of words and deliberate selection of words for precise meaning, create mood and atmosphere
- Use of different sentence lengths to vary pace and create specific effects
- Experiment with, evaluate and use a range of literary techniques, drawn from reading, for impact; for example, alliteration, onomatopoeia, metaphor
- Independent development of their own success criteria or toolkits
- Have regular writing conversations throughout the writing process with a focus on evaluating the impact of writing and using the redrafting process effectively
- Undertake independent editing and proof reading skills

(c) Focus Education (UK) Ltd

FOCUS EDUCATION

Year 6

(c) Focus Education (UK) Ltd

Year 6 Writers at Greater depth

Year 6 writers at greater depth have consistently met the Y6 writing expectations over a period of time and in a range of writing for different purposes and readers. Writers will make their own choices about the purpose and audience. All writing has a clear purpose and audience with the reader successfully engaged. They also show the individual "voice" and style of the pupil as a writer. Shorter pieces are well-crafted for impact and longer pieces are sustained and consistent. Writing is carefully structured and organised according to its context. Paragraphs successfully guide the reader through the text and are shaped and developed to ensure cohesion. Endings are clear and linked to openings dependent on the text type. Word choices are precise and selected for the purpose and audience. The use of sentences is controlled and a range of structures are used to create specific effects. Literary devices are well-chosen and used appropriately to create intended effects. Punctuation is accurate and used to clarify meaning. Spelling is consistently accurate and handwriting is fluent, joined and legible with a developed personal style.

Pupils need to meet the statements in the 2017-2018 assessment framework on the following page.

(c) Focus Education (UK) Ltd

2017-2018 Assessment Frameworks

Working at the expected standard	Working at greater depth
The pupil can: • write effectively for a range of purposes and audiences, selecting language that shows good awareness of the reader (e.g. the use of the first person in a diary; direct address in instructions and persuasive writing) • in narratives, describe settings, characters and atmosphere • integrate dialogue in narratives to convey character and advance the action • select vocabulary and grammatical structures that reflect what the writing requires, doing this mostly appropriately (e.g. using contracted forms in dialogues in narrative; using passive verbs to affect how information is presented; using modal verbs to suggest degrees of possibility) • use a range of devices to build cohesion (e.g. conjunctions, adverbials of time and place, pronouns, synonyms) within and across paragraphs • use verb tenses consistently and correctly throughout their writing • use the range of punctuation taught at key stage 2 mostly correctly (e.g. inverted commas and other punctuation to indicate direct speech) • spell correctly most words from the year 5 / year 6 spelling list, and use a dictionary to check the spelling of uncommon or more ambitious vocabulary • maintain legibility in joined handwriting when writing at speed.	The pupil can: • write effectively for a range of purposes and audiences, selecting the appropriate form and drawing independently on what they have read as models for their own writing (e.g. literary language, characterisation, structure) • distinguish between the language of speech and writing and choose the appropriate register • exercise an assured and conscious control over levels of formality, particularly through manipulating grammar and vocabulary to achieve this • use the range of punctuation taught at key stage 2 correctly (e.g. semi-colons, dashes, colons, hyphens) and, when necessary, use such punctuation precisely to enhance meaning and avoid ambiguity. [There are no additional statements for spelling or handwriting]

The Story of the Trojan Horse

Curiosity was my only motivation, but it was still enough to drive me out of my bed. Silently, I tip-toed out of my room, down the stairs, right down to the front door. Finally, I was out of the house.

A smell of freshly varnished now surrounded me. Calm yourself, I told myself crossly. It shouldn't be the only thing on ~~you're~~ your mind. But it was. The gargantuan, outstanding horse, which had earlier been surrounded by Trojans, was now free for me to look at. In utter silence, I watched this statuesque beast; an impossibly grand building in Troy! Clean, flawless wood reflected a starry night sky. Garlands of flowers crowned it. Troy's riches lay at its' feet.

Suddenly, a dark thought crossed my mind. What if it was all a lie. The Greeks could have just sailed out of sight. And to my horror, I found

twinkl.co.uk

I was right. About a dozen Greek soldiers clambered out from under a concealed trapdoor. Silently, they lowered themselves down a thickly knotted rope. "Quickly!" a sentry hissed.

The Greeks marched out. They were powerful, heavily armored soldiers; grim-faced and heavily ferocious. And since the Greeks were thought to be gone, there were no guards on duty. Troy didn't stand a chance.

Thoughts flashed through my head; what can I do? what shall I do? But then, I watched a tiny flame rise into a blazing inferno. All that is ~~teft~~ left of Troy is a large, wooden horse.

twinkl.co.uk

A precise and finely crafted text which has a clear voice and which creates mood and atmosphere. Tension is effectively built and the reader lulled into a false sense of security with an extended descriptive paragraph. The opening hooks the reader and establishes viewpoint which is sustained throughout the piece. The closing rounds off the text in an understated way, leaving the reader to picture the final scene.

Paragraphing is used extremely effectively to engage and interest the reader as well as to ensure cohesion across the text.

Sentences are varied and well-constructed and controlled. There are short sentences which create impact and tension and multi-clause sentences which convey more detail and complicated information clearly and effectively.

The use of the first person also adds to the clear viewpoint and allows the emotional aspect of the text to be expressed simply and effectively.

Word choices are precise, deliberate and thoughtful and verb forms used accurately. A range of literary features are used to create the planned effect; for example, short sentences, rhetorical questions.

Writing is accurate with the use of the comma secure and the semi-colon used to mark the boundary between clauses.

Working with Year 6 potential greater depth writers:

- Encourage wide reading and make explicit links and connections with other reading experiences
- Discuss the use of language and word choices made by the writer and collect examples for use in writing
- Widen range of different writers' styles and techniques investigated, discussed and used as a base for writing.
- Encourage independent adaptation of the features of different text types for the purpose or audience for the writing
- Discuss and identify the viewpoint for writing and sustain it through texts
- Develop understanding of the range of language on an informal to formal continuum and when and how different registers may be used
- Develop understanding of how a text may have different levels of informal and formal language and how to sustain the level or move from one to the other
- Understand and experiment with different verb forms and control them within multi-clause sentences
- Encourage independent exploration of words and deliberate selection of words for precise meaning, create mood and atmosphere
- Use semi-colons and colons to mark clause boundaries and control sentence structure for clarity
- Experiment with, evaluate and use a range of literary techniques which can be used, for example, to build tension, add pace, create mood, reinforce a point of view
- Independent development of their own success criteria or toolkits
- Have regular writing conversations throughout the writing process with a focus on evaluating the impact of writing and using the redrafting process effectively
- Undertake independent editing and proof reading skills

(c) Focus Education (UK) Ltd

Working towards the end of KS2 assessment

(c) Focus Education (UK) Ltd

The key aspects currently required to evidence pupils who are working at greater depth within the expected standard are the following:

"The pupil can:

- **write effectively for a range of purposes and audiences, selecting the appropriate form and drawing independently on what they have read as models for their own writing (e.g. literary language, characterisation, structure)**
- **distinguish between the language of speech and writing and choose the appropriate register**
- **exercise an assured and conscious control over levels of formality, particularly through manipulating grammar and vocabulary to achieve this**
- **use the range of punctuation taught at key stage 2 correctly (e.g. semi-colons, dashes, colons, hyphens) and, when necessary, use such punctuation precisely to enhance meaning and avoid ambiguity."**

We need to begin to address these elements throughout KS2, not just in Year 6. Pupils need time to read and identify examples in reading, experiment with using them in writing and to evaluate their effectiveness.

(c) Focus Education (UK) Ltd

Punctuation

Semi-colons

They separate two main clauses that are closely related to each other but could stand on their own as sentences if you wanted them to.

I have an important test tomorrow; I can't go out tonight.

They give the writer variety and control.

The moon was gleaming silver; it looked like an enormous lantern.

When a conjunctive adverb or an adverbial phrase is used. For example, however, therefore, for example, on the other hand.

The rain forest is being destroyed; as a result, many animals have become endangered.

(c) Focus Education (UK) Ltd

Colon

Joins two separate sentences/independent clauses and adds further explanation to a point previously made.

The climate is undergoing changes: summers are wetter and cooler and the sun rarely shines.

(c) Focus Education (UK) Ltd

Find examples of the effective use of colons and semi-colons in reading. Discuss and evaluate the use.

Good examples can be used as models for children to write their own sentences or paragraphs. This process will act as scaffolding towards independent use of the punctuation in children's own writing.

See following example.

Spot the uses

One by one, the familiar sounds of the morning drew Tashi from her sleep. Her mother breathing life into the fire; the hiss and crackle of the twigs as the flames caught; the whispering of the soot-blackened kettle as the water came to the boil. Tashi took her bowl of sweet tea outside and stood by the rough road in the blue morning.
The sun had not yet found a way through the mountains, but it was coming; a light the colour of lemons was soaking into the sky and painting out the stars. The air was very cold. Tashi shivered and pulled her shawl more tightly around herself. As the stars went out, small squares of light appeared on the dark hillside above her: lamps were being lit in the village.

These writers need to be very clear that the use of punctuation is to make their meaning clear.

The proof reading process will allow them to read aloud their own writing and check that there is clarity and that the meaning is not ambiguous.

Playing with sentences can help to raise the profile of the importance of punctuation. For example, the positioning of commas:

After we left Sam Annie and I went swimming.
The children who got ice cream were very happy.
James likes cooking his dog and his family.
My aunt collects many things: gold paper cups and hat pins.
Most of the time travellers worry about their luggage.
Some children were eating friends walking beside them.

(c) Focus Education (UK) Ltd

Understanding register and controlling levels of formality

(c) Focus Education (UK) Ltd

Understanding register and levels of formality

First understand the continuum of formality…

Children need to understand that there are varying degrees of formality and informality (register). The degree of formality will depend on the context. All pupils need to experience and understand the different registers of language as they all need to be able to sustain the register in their writing. For example, in a formal argument.

The first step is to use oracy to support this understanding.

It may be useful to display a continuum and use it to develop understanding of the different level of language and as an on-going reference.

Language can be collected, discussed and placed on the continuum.

A continuum of classroom talk

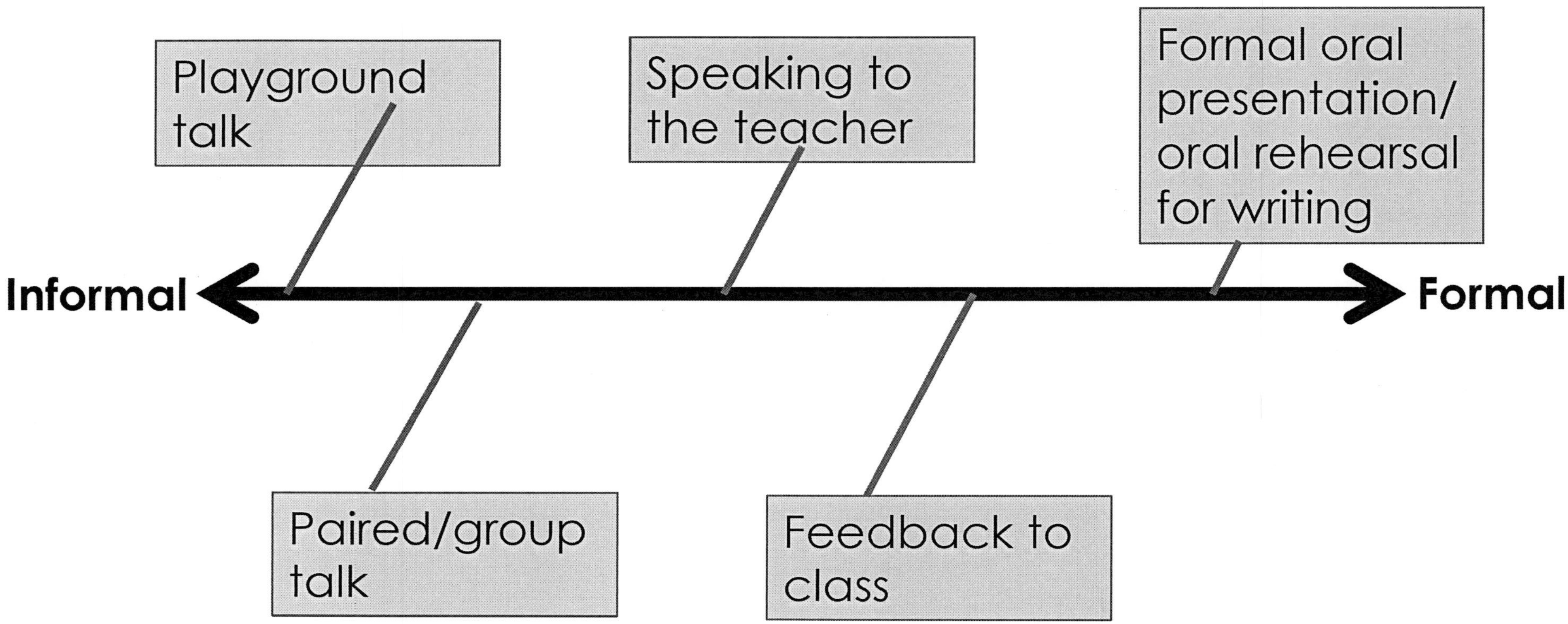

A continuum of greetings, for example

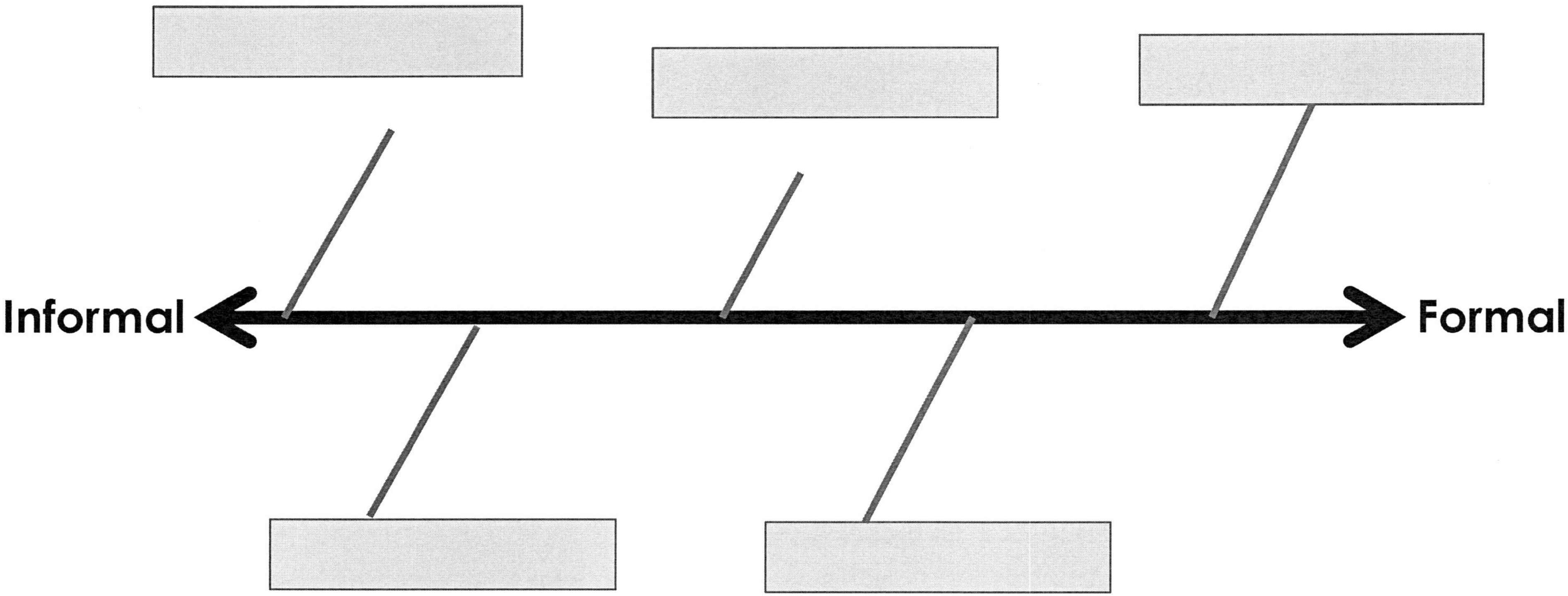

A continuum of greetings

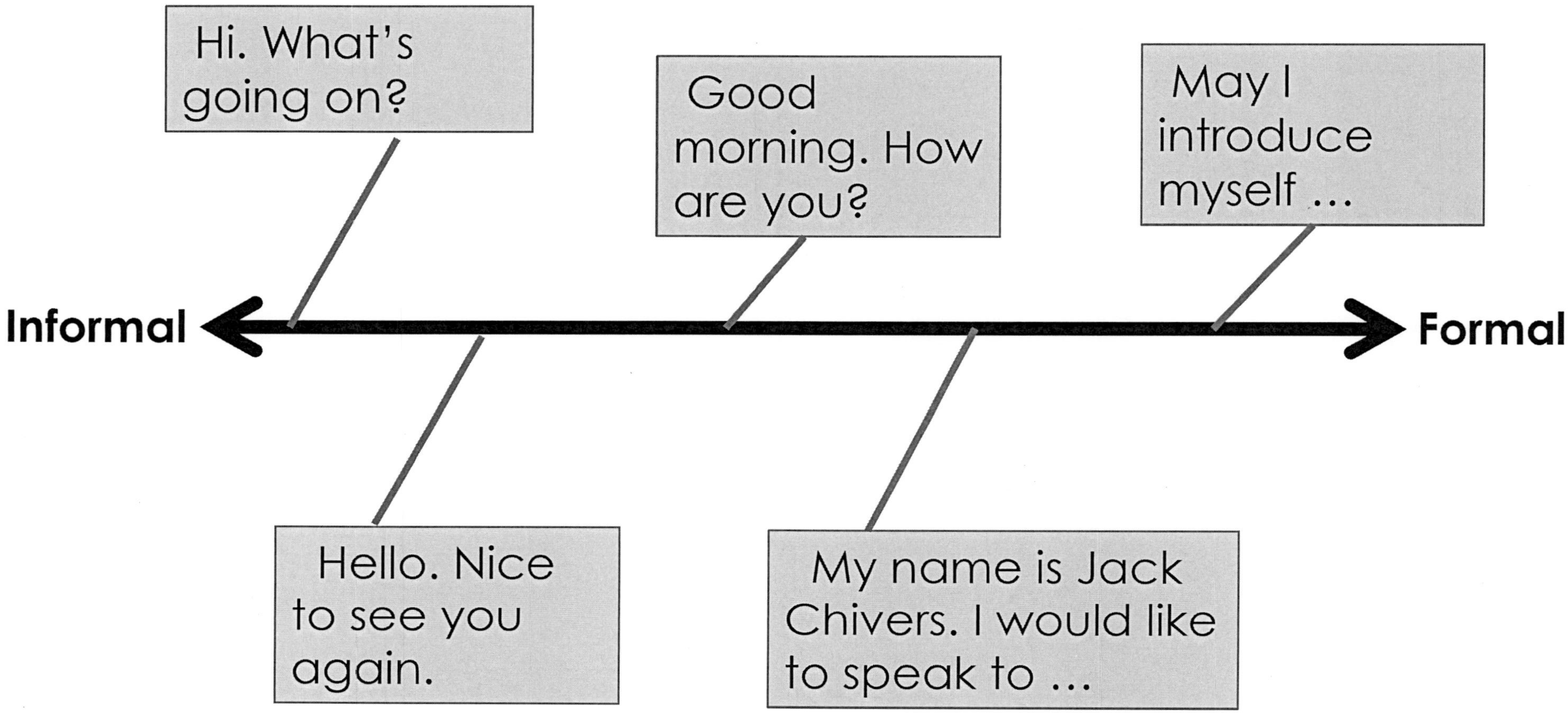

(c) Focus Education (UK) Ltd

Children need to identify register in the texts they are reading. They need to gather examples of formal and informal language and explore how and why writers use this language.

Language can be ranked along the same continuum from very informal to the most formal.

"Holes", "Wonder", "The Watertower", "Trash", "The Lost Thing" are just a few of the books which show appropriate use of and control over register and the levels of formality as real writers would use them.

This experience is essential in order for children to be able to use the appropriate register and control and maintain appropriate levels of formality in their own writing.

(c) Focus Education (UK) Ltd

Using texts – The Lost Thing by Shaun Tan

Informal ⟷ Formal

"I dunno, man," said Pete.

"I have a lost thing," I called to the receptionist at the front desk. "Fill in these forms."

This book is intended to serve as an introductory text book for students.

"It could have all kinds of strange diseases," warned Dad.

As the hours slouched by, it seemed less and less likely that anybody was coming to take the thing home.

(c) Focus Education (UK) Ltd

What to look for:

Formal features	Informal features
• Modality • Use of passive voice • Use of subjunctive mood • Precise/technical vocabulary • Verb choices and forms • Punctuation choice – semi-colon or colon to mark clause boundaries	• Contracted verb forms • Slang • Colloquial language • Abbreviations • Question tags • Conversational language/tone • Punctuation choices – use of dash to mark clause boundaries

Using verb choices to support register and control writing:

- Consistency of tense
- Subject-verb agreement
- Modal and auxiliary verbs used appropriately to indicate certainty or uncertainty, likelihood, possibility
- Passive voice in different contexts.
- Contracted forms – these could be simply **isn't** or could indicate the use of the present perfect - **Jack's lost** his book or the present progressive – **Daniel's staring**.
- Confident control of verbs in multi-clause sentences - **The clouds had grown darker and they were now piling up in great heaps, alerting Lily to the fact that she would have to find shelter soon.**

The following pages offer some practical approaches to working with verbs.

(c) Focus Education (UK) Ltd

Experimenting with modals

You can live a contented life.
You may live a contented life.
You will live a contented life.
You should live a contented life.
You ought to live a contented life.
You must live a contented life.
You could live a contented life.

- which is most likely?
- which is least likely?

(c) Focus Education (UK) Ltd

Using modal adverbs

possibly
probably
certainly
definitely
unquestionably
absolutely
perhaps
surely
maybe
without doubt

Add an adverb …

(c) Focus Education (UK) Ltd

…and make your point of view stronger

Surely you can live a contented life.

… you should live a contented life.

… you ought to live a contented life.

… you could live a contented life.

(c) Focus Education (UK) Ltd

Past perfect tense

Past Perfect

When I **had chosen** the threads

Simple Past

I **began** to weave.

Past → **Present**

It **had been** her desire to become an enchantress that **had brought** her to this sorry state.

(c) Focus Education (UK) Ltd

Building multi-clause sentences

Offer models for children to change and manipulate.

Twigs snapped and leaves rustled as he sprinted through the misty trees, panting with fear and exhaustion.

The road had become narrow and the hedges on either side were thick and tangled, warning Joe that the turning he was seeking would not be easy to find.

(c) Focus Education (UK) Ltd

Using the passive voice

S V O

The police are following a number of leads.

S V

A number of leads are being followed by the police.

S V O

The police interviewed a suspect.

(c) Focus Education (UK) Ltd

Active sentence	**Passive sentence**
Officials searched the dumpsite at Behala.	
The police arrested a dumpsite boy.	
They released him after interrogation.	

(c) Focus Education (UK) Ltd

Sorting the subjunctive

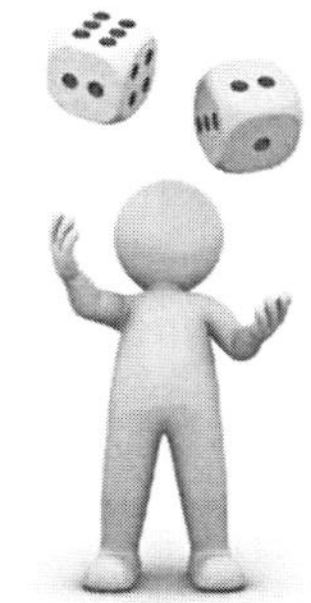

Expressing wishes or possibilities:

If .... were ...., ... would ....

If Mr Spider were so heartless, he would not have wined and dined Miss Flytingale so lavishly.

If I were .... , I would ....

Making commands more formal

The court expects that the jury be attentive.

The judge requires that .... be ....

The defence insists that .... be ....

The prosecution demands that .... be ....

Where understanding of register and controlling of levels of formality can be demonstrated:

- To show the writer's thoughts and feelings. For example, informal personal comments that may directly address the reader in a more formal report of discursive text
- Fact and opinion interwoven in an information or discursive text
- The use of dialogue in narrative writing to show characterisation – more formal language used to address an authority figure and informal chat between friends or family
- Quotes in a more formal text
- Explicit changes within a text – informal anecdotes, an extract from live commentary of an event inserted in a more formal report after the event, letter to more than one recipient – parent, sibling

(c) Focus Education (UK) Ltd

- Newspaper reports – eye-witness quotes will be informal whilst the report itself will use formal language.
- Diary entries – may include informal personal comments and more formal narration of an event.
- Recount text on a subject of personal interest – more formal explanation of the subject and more informal personal response to it.
- An event narrated in different forms – email, text, note, letter for example.
- Discursive texts – statistics and impersonal, generalised language with personal comment, rhetorical questions with question tags, concluding personal view
- Flashback in a narrative – informal to formal or vice versa
- Foreshadowing in a narrative – shift to more informal language

Developing the Editing Process

(c) Focus Education (UK) Ltd

Editing – improving the quality and impact of writing - needs to be explicitly taught as a skill and a vital part of the writing process. It also needs to be kept apart from checking for accuracy – proof reading.

Both processes should develop through both key stages and sufficient time and guidance given to children in order to edit and proof read effectively. This may be that a specific sentence, a specific paragraph or a particular aspect is identified or the success criteria or toolkit offers clear guidance.

It is important that the children understand that when they are writing their first draft, their concentration must be on composition and that they will have time to go back and improve and check later. Writers can lose the "flow" of their writing if they are trying to compose, improve and check at the same time.

The following pages offer practical strategies and approaches to introduce and establish effective and thoughtful editing and proof reading.

(c) Focus Education (UK) Ltd

On a practical note ...

Children need space in their books to edit and proof read their writing. For significant pieces of writing, it can be useful to leaving the facing page blank which leaves ample space for children to write in their edits whether it is a word, phrase, sentence or entire paragraph.

Strips of paper – editing flaps – can also be used. Children write their edited or changes on the flap and then stick the left hand side of the strip in the book so that it covers the word or section that has been changed. The flap can then be lifted to see the original and the child's changes.

Read aloud

Writing should be read aloud firstly to evaluate whether or not the writing flows, sounds good and maintains interest. Following improvements, it should be read aloud to check for accuracy.

This is a strategy that can be used from KS1. Paired work can be useful here and there are different approaches:

- Peer critique
- Response partner
- Writing partner
- Critical friend

Whatever approach is used or what it is called, children need to be taught how to work with each other, how to listen to each other and they need the appropriate language to do so.

A routine can be put into place so that children become used to reading their work aloud and understand that this is an important part of the writing process.

Key understandings:

- Be positive and articulate
- Be specific and give a helpful comment

(c) Focus Education (UK) Ltd

Making the language explicit

Positive

I like the way you …
I was engaged by your writing because …
What stood out for me was …
My favourite part was …
It was effective when you …

Suggesting improvements

Next time, try …
How about if you …
Have you thought about …
Why don't you try …
Could you consider …

Start with a sentence

Use a good example taken from one of the children's writing and display it. It is more effective to use a well-written example to show children how even this can be improved.

- Begin by explaining that it is a good sentence
- Highlight or underline the parts of the sentence that they like as a whole class
- Identify where improvements could be made:
  - change a word to make it more precise
  - take out redundant, unnecessary or over-elaborate language
  - add words, phrases, clauses within the sentence to add detail/create an image for the reader
  - add a word, phrase or clause to the beginning or end of the sentence
  - change the order of the sentence
  - include a literary technique – imagery, for example
- Experiment with improvements on whiteboards and decide on whole class version
- In pairs/individually write own improved version of the original sentence

Children can choose a sentence from their own writing, or one identified by the teacher, to improve. Peer working is useful here too so that they are testing their sentences out with each other.

(c) Focus Education (UK) Ltd

Moving on...

Move from focusing on one sentence to two sentences and then a sequence of sentences or a paragraph, depending on the year group of the children, using the same process.

Guide the children to improve one aspect of a paragraph or longer text. This should be part of the success criteria, learning focus, toolkit. For example:

- Joining ideas or information with appropriate conjunctions
- Expanded noun phrases to add detail and make a picture in the reader's head
- Fronted adverbials to mark changes
- Word choices to engage the reader
- Suitability of word choices/language for the purpose and audience

Always focus the children on impact on the reader!

(c) Focus Education (UK) Ltd

Editing stations

Editing stations can be used during or after the writing process. They allow us to guide children into looking at specific aspects of their writing rather than improving or checking an extended text for everything. They can be used firstly to improve writing. Once this completed, stations can be set up to proof read.

Tables are set up around the room with each table having a specific focus:

- Use of the passive voice
- Topic sentence to open paragraphs
- Expanded noun phrases to add detail
- Use of relative clause
- Direct speech to show character

Or proof reading

- Capital letters and end marks
- Specific common exception words
- Semi-colon to mark boundaries
- Use of inverted commas

(c) Focus Education (UK) Ltd

Editing stations

Children move from station to station and focus on the aspect on the station. They will work in pairs to find an example of the identified aspect in their own writing and discuss whether it has been used effectively or accurately and how it could be improved if necessary or corrected.

Prompts and modelling are helpful:

- Can you find a passive sentence? Why did you use it there? Does the writing flow?
- Find a paragraph and the topic sentence. Does it introduce the paragraph? How could it be improved?
- Can you find a spelling you think might not be right? How can we check it?

(c) Focus Education (UK) Ltd